I REMEMBER WHEN...
THEN AND NOW

When I was Your age?

EVANGELINE T. MOORE

AuthorHouse™
1663 Liberty Drive
Bloomington, IN 47403
www.authorhouse.com
Phone: 833-262-8899

Because of the dynamic nature of the Internet, any web addresses or links contained in this book may have changed since publication and may no longer be valid. The views expressed in this work are solely those of the author and do not necessarily reflect the views of the publisher, and the publisher hereby disclaims any responsibility for them.

Any people depicted in stock imagery provided by Getty Images are models, and such images are being used for illustrative purposes only.
Certain stock imagery © Getty Images.

This book is printed on acid-free paper.

ISBN: 978-1-6655-6481-6 (sc)
ISBN: 978-1-6655-6480-9 (e)

Library of Congress Control Number: 2022913115

Print information available on the last page.

Published by AuthorHouse 07/14/2022

authorHOUSE

Dedication Page

in loving memory of my
parents, James and Cassie

I remember when children said yes ma'am, no ma'am and yes sir, no sir to adults. Now some say yeah, yep, nope and what!

I remember when we had to make up our beds before coming out of the room to brush our teeth. Now some throw the coverings back and leave it.

I remember when My sister and I shared a room with twin beds. A dresser was between the beds. My side of the dresser had a small plastic toy dresser where I kept my hair bows.

Now I sleep in a king size bed.

I remember when we ate dinner at the table together as a family. The food was blessed before we ate. Now some eat at all different times, in their rooms, or watching tv.

I remember when there was only one tv in the house. Now there's a tv in every room even the kitchen.

I Remember when going to school was important and it didn't matter how far you had to walk. Now the bus picks up right outside the house. Children wore their best to school. Now some wear uniforms.

I Remember when children were not aloud to sit in adult company. We had to play outside. If we heard adults talking, we couldn't repeat or look at the person talking. It was be seen and not heard. Now children join the conversation.

I Remember when at church, if children misbehaved, mothers would give a stern look from across the room and we straightened up. Now, some children say what you lookin at?

I remember when the country store had candy, cookies, and gas. A quarter would get you a 16 ounce bottle of soda, a bag of chips and ten cookies. Now a cookie cost more than a quarter.

I Remember when aprons were worn in the kitchen to wash dishes or cook? Now dishwashers do a lot of the work.

I remember when there were chores before and after school. Now children spend afternoons playing sports, practicing karate, and other activities.

I Remember when children played outside all day long until dinner time. Now they spend all day inside sitting at a computer or holding electronics in their hands.

I remember when toys were made out of wood and tin. Now most are made of plastic.

I remember birthday dinners were fried chicken, collard greens, potato salad and a cake cooked from scratch with homemade icing. Today we go out to eat at our favorite restaurant.

I remember when dropping out of school was not an option because our parents wanted us to have a better life than they did. When each one of us graduated from high school, we were given a set of luggage to carry with us where ever our dreams would take us.

21

The End

Written by Evangeline Moore

Printed in the United States
by Baker & Taylor Publisher Services